Introduction..................
Marathon Training .....
Marathon Nutrition ..../
Marathon Gear..14
Marathon Mentality 20
Marathon Racing 24
Marathon Recovery 36
Thank You 41

Introduction

If you're reading this book, chances are you're at least considering a marathon this year. That's how it begins. It's like a little voice that gets louder as the days go by until it finally screams "You can do this!" Then, after hours of contemplation and research, you hold your breath as you submit your race registration.

`Registration confirmed.` You'll feel a sudden wave of euphoria that is quickly eclipsed by a stomach-turning wave of self-doubt as the implications of marathon training sink in. You'll worry about the freakishly long training runs. You'll recall in great detail the marathon horror stories you've heard from other runners. And, you may feel guilty about the sacrifices your family will make to get you to the starting line. Not to worry, it's normal.

Don't let the nerves and the worries consume you. You are a runner. You laugh in the face of fear. You enjoy the long miles of torment, because you know they are making you stronger. You run while others sit still.

You are about to embark on a journey of empowerment and self-discovery that very few people experience in their lifetime. You are about to discover an even better version of YOU!

Ready? Let's do this!

1
Marathon Training

Training for your first marathon isn't about being fast or slow. It's about completing the race and finishing in an upright position with a smile plastered across your face. You don't need a fancy training plan with tempo runs, track workouts, hills, and strides. You just need to build your endurance and enjoy the transformation from runner to endurance athlete.

Find a training plan developed by an experienced coach that is made for a beginner like you. Then, trust the plan. If you follow the plan, you'll finish the race. Really. Your new running body is an incredibly adaptive machine. You can transform from a 6-mile runner to a 26-mile runner in just 4 months.

Marathon training is hard. You'll have days where you just can't muster the energy or find the time to complete your workout. No problem. If you miss a workout from time to time, you're human. It's the quality of the overall approach to training that matters most.

Each week consists of several runs. The long run is the workout that matters most. This is the one you don't want to skip unless your sick or injured. If it falls on a Sunday and you're busy, move it to Saturday. As coach Bill Squires says, "The long run is what puts the tiger in the cat."

If you're the kind of person who finds energy and motivation by running with others, look for a local running club or running specialty store that hosts group runs. You'll not only enjoy some friendly conversation, but you'll learn a lot from the other runners. Be sure to pick a pace group that works for you.

Stretching and mobility work will help keep your body limber and reduce your chances of injury. I recommend a quick routine of dynamic stretches before each run, some static stretching after a run, and mobility work before bedtime. If you treat your body well, it will return the favor on race day.

Strength training can help improve your running form and ward off injury, but approach this area carefully. If you're working hard to complete a tough training schedule, introducing additional strength training can sometimes hurt more than it helps.

Training Plans

You can find training plans online or in the bookstore. They all follow roughly the same progression. Many beginners have found success using the training plans developed by Hal Higdon and Jeff Galloway. If you're signed up for a large marathon like NYC or Chicago, you may find free training plans on their websites.

My First Marathon Training Plan – 16 weeks

(http://saltmarshrunning.com/wp-content/uploads/2015/01/MyFirstMarathonTPlan.pdf)

Hal Higdon's Marathon Novice Supreme – 30 weeks

(http://www.halhigdon.com/training/51143/Marathon-Novice-Supreme-Training-Program)

Jeff Galloway's Marathon to Finish – 30 weeks

(http://www.jeffgalloway.com/training/marathon-training/)

New York Road Runners Club Conservative Guide – 16 weeks

(http://www.nyrr.org/sites/default/files/Marathon%20Training%20Plans%20-%20Conservative.pdf)

Expert Tip: If you're tired and sore, it's okay take a day off.

2
Marathon Nutrition

One of the side benefits of marathon training is eating– a lot. You'll be burning calories and exhausting your body like crazy, and that requires a steady stream of top-notch high quality fuel. Marathon runners need to eat plenty of healthy natural foods and stay hydrated by drinking plenty of water. And, to keep the tank from running dry on a long run, runners need to learn how to eat and drink while racing.

Healthy Food Choices for Runners

Bill Rodgers, winner of 4 Boston Marathons and 4 NYC Marathons, once said that "If the furnace is hot enough, anything will burn, even Big Macs." I wouldn't suggest a diet of Big Macs or running 140-160 miles each week as Rodgers did. But, it's definitely OK to give yourself a treat every now and then. That's part of the marathon training fun.

For the most part, a runner's diet should consist of healthy foods. Avoid processed foods and eat real foods. Real foods are foods that you make from fresh ingredients, or foods that were once growing before they reached your table. Avoid processed foods.

Processed foods are foods that you microwave or pop in the oven for a quick fix. Processed foods are kept in plastic wrappers and sit on shelves for years at a time. They contain preservatives, sugars, fats, and chemicals that are good for shelf-life, but terrible for you.

Your running diet should consist of a variety of fresh fruits and vegetables, whole grains, and healthy cuts of poultry, meat or fish. As you begin your training you'll marvel at how your body and mind work together to support your training by craving healthy foods. For most runners, healthy snacking throughout the day is a good way to keep energy levels steady and fuel the furnace.

Protein is important for muscle growth and recovery. Many runners will use supplements to make sure that they are getting enough protein during marathon training.

Whey protein is recommended for runners and can easily be added to smoothies and drinks in powdered form.

Running Super Foods

- Almonds
- Avocado
- Bananas
- Beans
- Beets
- Blueberries
- Chicken
- Eggs
- Greek Yogurt
- Lentils
- Pasta
- Peanut Butter
- Red Bell Pepper
- Salmon
- Spinach
- Sweet Potatoes

- Swiss Chard
- Tuna Fish
- Turkey Breast
- Whole Grain Brown Rice

Carbohydrate Loading Before the Marathon

Even non-runners know that marathoners love their spaghetti dinners. I prefer my wife's homemade Chicken Parmesan, but the carbo-loading theory is still the same. And, while many think it's a one-time feast the night before a race, it actually takes several days to carbo-load for the marathon.

To understand how carbohydrate loading works, you first need to know that carbohydrates are converted to glycogen by the body and stored for use as energy by your muscles. Years ago, carbohydrate loading included a hard workout followed by a 3-day phase of an extremely low carb diet to deplete glycogen stores, and then a 3-day phase of carbohydrate rich foods to create an extra high level of glycogen storage for race day. Today, most coaches and runners agree that to minimize risk of injury or poor health, runners really only need to follow the last 3 days of the carbo-loading ritual prior to the marathon.

Two important things to keep in mind during carbo-loading time. First, this isn't license to eat whatever you want. Smothering your pasta in Alfredo sauce and Italian sausage is not a healthy approach. Eating a simple tomato sauce with fresh vegetables over a bed of pasta is a more sensible choice. Second, this is a time to choose white pasta over the more healthy and fiber-rich brown pasta. Your body can digest the white pasta faster and it's less likely to cause stomach upset on race day.

Fueling On the Run to Avoid "The Wall"

Have you experienced the "bonk" or the "wall" on a long run? Most endurance athletes know the feeling all too well. Your fuel tank runs dry, your glycogen stores are depleted, and your run turns into something resembling a forced march to the finish line. For me, it happened at the 2013 New York City Marathon. Things were fine until I hit the wall at mile 20.

To make it to the finish, you'll need a solid fueling strategy that you've thoroughly tested during your long training runs. You can try Clif Shots, GU gels, Island Boost, Honey Stinger, Gatorade chews, EnergyBits, or a dozen other commercial products. My friend Tim swears by Swedish Fish, while my friend Kate loves to munch on gummy bears and waffles. Olympic marathon winner, Frank Shorter used to drink flat Coke during his races.

The point is, there is no one perfect way to fuel during your race. But, whatever method you choose must be tested or you may suffer gastrointestinal consequences on race day. A good rule of thumb is the 1-hour rule. If you are running for more than an hour, you really need to eat something. so, once your long runs creep up to the 60-minute mark, you should begin carrying some gels or snacks with you.

You'll want to have the first one about 40 minutes into you run, followed by another every 30 minutes. You should also plan on drinking a few gulps of water every 20 minutes or so. If you are eating, that usually means you should be drinking. Many of the gels and chews need water to dissolve and enter your bloodstream faster. Be careful not to drink a sports drink like Gatorade Endurance with your gels, it will make digestion difficult.

So how do you carry snacks and water with you on your training runs? You could buy a belt with tons of pockets and little water bottles attached to it. You could run with a hydration pack on your back. Or, you could stash water bottles and snacks along your route before you leave the house on your run.

Personally, I can't stand the extra weight of a belt or a hydration pack. If I'm in the mountains or on the trail maybe, but on the roads I'd rather take the time to stash my stuff and turn my run into an Easter egg hunt. The drawback is that it takes extra time before and after the run to drive around. Especially if you're running 20 miles or more.

You may also want to consider repeating some smaller course loops closer to home. This allows you to use your home as an aid station, medical tent, or early exit if necessary. It will also gives your family members piece of mind to see you every so often during a long training run.

A Successful Marathon Fueling Strategy

1. Find out what the race is supplying at aid stations (gels brands, water, sports drink)
2. Try these things out and see if they work for you on training runs
3. On race day choose energy drinks at each station unless you are eating something or have an upset stomach.
4. Grab a drink by mile 3 or 4 even if you don't think you need it yet.
5. Have your first energy snack by 45 minutes. Follow up every 30-45 minutes with another.

Expert Tip: After the race drink plenty of water and eat some protein and carbohydrates. Marathons usually supply runners with a healthy snack mix that fits this nutritional need perfectly. Resist the temptation to drink alcohol until you've had at least a few glasses of water.

3
Marathon Gear

Buying the Perfect Running Shoes

Choosing the right running shoes and gear is extremely important for runners. The wrong shoes can lead to injury, discomfort, or end your running career before it begins. However, choosing the right shoe will keep your feet happy, support your unique running mechanics, and make the miles fly by.

1. **Foot Type and Gait Analysis**

We all have unique physical attributes. The first step to finding the right pair of running shoes is to determine your individual needs. Do you have flat feet or high arches? Do you pronate or supinate? Are you a heel-striker? These are difficult questions, especially for beginners. Fortunately, there are experts available (at no cost) to analyze your specific needs and point you in the right direction. Find your local running specialty store and pay them a visit. Or, research your shoes using credible running shoe review sites.

2. **Don't Believe the Hype**

Be careful not to get caught up in the marketing hype that shoe companies use to sell their products. Barefoot running, spring-loaded blades, energy return lugs, extra

thin soles, extra thick soles, etc. They all claim to be innovative and new, which makes them risky choices. You can be cutting edge, but bleeding edge isn't cool. Go with something that's been validated by thousands of other runners.

3. Comfort Over Style

Once you know the type of shoe you need, the fun begins. Try on as many shoes as you can. When you find a shoe that feels good, you'll know it right away. Your running shoes should provide plenty of wiggle room for your toes while remaining snug around your heel. Hopefully, you find a shoe that looks as good as it feels.

4. Run Before Buying

Run in your shoes before purchasing them. Most specialty stores will allow you to take a quick run in their shoes before you buy them. If you purchase online, look for companies that will allow you to return them after taking them out of the box for a run. The run test should be done at your regular running pace to determine fit and feel.

Buying the Perfect Running Gear

The gear you purchase has to be a good match for the environment you run in. Winter running is challenging, but enjoyable if you choose the right gear. Summer running is also a challenge, but let's face it, there is only so much you can take off before people start complaining.

When shopping for gear consider form and function first, and style second. Is this jacket waterproof and windproof? Does this shirt have flat seams for comfort? Do these shorts have pockets for my gels? is there enough reflective material on these running tights for drivers to see me on my early morning runs? Does this hat breathe so that I won't sweat too much and get chilled?

One thing is for sure. No matter how much gear you have, you'll always want more. Here's a list of gear to consider for each season of the year. This list is based on a northern climate, so adjust accordingly.

Summer

- running shoes – rotate 2 pairs
- ankle socks – 3
- shorts – 2

- singlet (tank) – 2
- technical t-shirt – 3
- visor/hat
- sunglasses
- sunscreen

Spring

- running shoes- rotate 2 pairs
- ankle socks – 3
- shorts – 2
- light running tights
- technical t-shirt – 3
- 3/4 zip or long sleeve running shirt
- light running jacket or wind-proof, water-proof shell
- visor/hat/beanie
- sunglasses
- sunscreen
- running gloves

Fall

- running shoes- rotate 2 pairs
- ankle socks – 3

- 3/4 socks Merino wool – 2
- shorts – 2
- light running tights
- technical t-shirt – 3
- 3/4 zip or long sleeve running shirt – 2
- light running jacket or wind-proof, water-proof shell
- visor/hat/beanie
- sunglasses
- sunscreen
- running gloves

Winter

- running shoes- rotate 2 pairs
- ankle socks – 2
- 3/4 socks Merino wool – 2
- wind-proof briefs
- shorts – 2
- light running tights
- heavy running tights
- technical t-shirt – 3
- insulated, breathable long-sleeve shirt – 2

- 3/4 zip or long sleeve running shirt
- light running jacket or wind-proof, water-proof shell
- visor/hat/beanie
- sunglasses
- sunscreen
- running gloves
- running mittens

Optional Gear

- Compression Socks
- Foam Roller
- GPS Watch

Expert Tip: As you compete in races, you'll pick up a lot of shirts along the way. Most of the gear lasts for years, but the shoes should be replaced every 400 miles.

4
Marathon Mentality

Beginning runners want to distract themselves from the effort of running. They blast music, bargain with themselves, and try to make it stop. More experienced runners realize that awareness and submission are essential parts of the running experience. As runners, we learn how to tune in to our own internal rhythms and block out external distractions.

Ask a marathoner to describer the scene during at a point during the first 5 miles of their race, and they will provide you with rich, vivid detail. Now ask them to do the same for miles 22 and 23 and see what they have to say. They will tell you that the shades were pulled low and they were fighting a battle with themselves, just trying to move forward one step at a time.

Distance running requires a disciplined mind and immense willpower. Fortunately, marathon training will develop both. As you begin to run longer distances, your mind will adapt to the tedium and repetitive task of running by entertaining itself.

"Much like the Bermuda Triangle, the runner's high is an elusive place that can't be found intentionally. Sometimes it doesn't appear at all. But when it does, I relish it. My most creative and inspiring ideas occur when I reach this point in a run. I see meaning in the most insignificant details. Minutes later, the spell breaks and my thoughts come back to the present. How much distance had I covered? A mile or two perhaps?"

During the race, your mind will keep track of pace, hunger, thirst, fatigue, signs of injury, fueling strategies, running form, and hundreds of other factors that go into running a successful marathon. Properly trained, your mind will slow you down in the beginning, monitor your effort levels midway through the race, and overrule your body's demands to stop as you cover the last few miles.

Training Your Mind to Become a Better Runner

Practice pace and learn what it feels like. If you know your pace by feel, it will make it easier to maintain over the course of the marathon. Running by effort is a more natural measure than running by time.

Focus on your breathing. Find a count that works for you. For example, a hard effort might be 2 steps in and 2 steps out. A marathon pace might be 3 steps in and 3 or 4 steps out. Everybody's different, but once you learn your rhythm it will help you stay on target.

Check your form. Are your feet landing under you? Are you slapping your feet or slamming your heels? Are your arms crossing your body too much? Are you standing up tall with your hips forward? Yes. No. No. Yes. Good.

Read the Fuel Gage. Is it time for a drink? Is it time for a snack? When is the last time you had something? What should you grab at the next aid station, water or sports drink?

Visualize Success. What are you going to do when you cross the finish line? What will the clock say? How will you feel? What will you wear on race day?

Stay positive. You can do this. Run the mile you're in now. Don't worry about what is coming up and how much farther you have to go.

Expert Tip: Often times a runner's perception of effort negatively affects their performance. Stay focused and keep pushing through the tough spots.

5
Marathon Racing

The final few weeks of training and the days leading up to your first marathon are going to put you on an emotional roller coaster ride, but you can find confidence in your training. Look over your training plan and think about everything you have done to get to this point. You have earned this chance at glory.

The Taper

The final phase of marathon training is called the taper. All of the miles and effort you put into preparation has left your body in a depleted and damaged state. The taper period allows for a full recovery while maintaining the benefits of prior training.

As your mileage dwindles, you may experience what I refer to as taper tantrums. The crazy mood swings that are caused by excessive energy coupled with anxiety and self-doubt. It's completely normal to feel this way, but as I said in training section, you have to trust the plan.

Carbohydrates, proteins and hydration are the three big components to eating well before your marathon. You want your body to be full of fuel and energy. Try to eat less fats, avoid junk, and consume less alcohol. You'll be burning fewer calories during the taper phase, so make each one count by eating healthy foods.

Planning

As race day gets closer, you'll want to consider all of your travel and lodging details to make sure that everything will be as easy as possible on race weekend. If you are making your race part of a larger family trip, be sure to plan for more than just the race. Keep in mind you are going to be in bed early the night before the race and sightseeing on foot will not be a part of your pre-race routine. And, after the race you'll want some quiet time followed by some easy walking and a lot of eating.

Bring your own food.

Eating healthy meals and race-friendly foods can be a challenge when traveling. Bring along some staples like bagels, pretzels, and fruit. Remember that security rules will prohibit you from bringing peanut butter, energy drinks, and some other food items. It may be a good idea to go shopping for a few of these things after you arrive.

Stick to your routine.

Be a creature of habit. Be sure to eat and sleep as you would at home. Not only will this make things easier on your children, but it will help minimize the disruption to your body's internal clock.

Don't walk too much.

This sounds like it might be an easy rule to follow, but it's one that I have struggled with more than any other. If you walk around the city to see the sights, you may be surprised how many miles you rack up over the course of the day. When I visited San Diego last year for the Rock 'n' Roll Half Marathon, I covered 12 miles the day before the race. Tough to run your best on tired legs.

Use your maps and apps.

Use your smartphone to make your life easier. Map out your destinations ahead of time. A bird's eye view of your location in real-time makes it easy if you get lost or need help finding your destination. You can even use a GPS app and follow the prompts as if you were in a car. I also depend upon apps like UrbanSpoon to help me find decent restaurants when I am in a new place. If you're a Twitter user, check out the hashtag for your race. Many times other runners are posting helpful pre and post-race suggestions.

Plan for your fans.

Your fans are the most important people in your life. Plan a vacation that you'd all enjoy even if the race is cancelled. On race day, pick out your post-race meeting locations and find some good cheering spots along the course. Seeing your family or friends along the race course will boost your spirits and make them a part of your fantastic 'racecation' experience.

Marathon Pacing

On race day if you go out too fast you'll end up paying a heavy toll for your foolish exuberance. The race may be 26.2 miles long, but it doesn't begin until mile 20.

1. Set a realistic goal and stick to the plan.

You have spent months training for this race. You know if you're on track to hit your goals based on your recent workouts. Now is not the time to be overly ambitious. Think about your fueling strategy, your race gear, your goal pace, and visualize success in meeting your goals on race day. When the cannon fires and the crowds cheer, be disciplined and stick to your race plan.

2. Steady as she goes.

Try your best to be consistent in your mile splits. If anything, you want your first miles to be slower than your last. There is nothing worse than running out of steam with 6 miles left to go. Check your pace every mile and adjust accordingly. The first half should be easy (green light), the next 7 a bit tougher but still not hard (yellow light), and the last 6 define your race.

There is no such thing as "time in the bank." You can't run 6:30 for the first 13.1, and assume that the next 13.1 will be an easy 7:30 pace, to result in an overall race pace of 7:00 per mile. It doesn't work that way. Your spending your retirement savings in your 20's and hoping it'll be fine. It won't be. The fatigue is cumulative and the miles get harder as you continue towards the finish line.

3. Adapt to the terrain.

If your marathon course isn't flat as a pancake, you'll have to account for a change in pace when you run up and down hills. Try to maintain the same level of effort as you run. You may slow down a bit on the inclines, but you'll also speed up a bit when you coast back down the other side. Be careful to give yourself enough wiggle room to account for terrain changes.

Each course is different. Do your research ahead of time by looking at the course maps, visiting the course for a preview, or by talking to others that have run the race before. If you're running Chicago, Boston, New York or any other big race, you'll find tons of information online to help you develop the right race strategy.

4. "Know when to walk away, know when to run."

Thank you Kenny Rogers for your marathon wisdom. Sometimes things just don't go well. Life happens. If it's not your day, and you know it before you hit the halfway point, consider shutting it down. You don't have to throw away your training. Count your effort as a tough workout, and sign up for the next marathon you see. Or, just walk and jog, and enjoy the spectacle of the marathon without the pressures of racing.

Bill Rodgers, 4-time winner of the New York City and Boston marathons, dropped out of the 1973 Boston Marathon at mile 21. He said "You want to be one of those runners who can succeed and not be in the medical tent after the race." (Yankee Magazine)

5. Where the mind goes, the body will follow.

The mental aspects of running a marathon would take entire volumes to cover adequately. Let's just say that to run 26.2 miles takes concentration, willpower, and extraordinary mental toughness. Tanzanian marathoner Juma Ikangaa once said "The will to win is nothing without the will to prepare." Toughness comes from training and believing in yourself.

Many runners have mantras that help them when the race becomes difficult. The Kenyan runners are known to use the phrase "Keep going, lion." Think about why you wanted to run a marathon in the first place, and that may help you come up with your own meaningful mantra to use on race day. Good mental discipline will help you stick to your pace and meet your race goals.

How to Run the Marathon Like a Pro

We all know that it takes some serious training to prepare your body for the rigors of a 26.2 mile race, but did you know your breakfast can make or break your race? I spoke with Andy Potts, 4th place finisher in this year's Ironman World Championship, about what it takes to make it through a grueling endurance race. His advice was simple and straight-forward, eat what agrees with you a couple of hours before the race.

For some it's eggs and bacon, for others it's a bowl of oatmeal. The essential takeaway is to eat something that you know won't cause you any stomach issues. The last thing you want to do before a race is eat something new, or grab race fuel that you've never tried before. Be predictable.

When it comes to race strategy, Gwen Jorgensen, the 2014 World Triathlon Series World Champion says stick to your plan. Go over your goals, determine your splits and fueling strategy and visualize the race. On race day, don't get carried away early in the race. Instead, remember your plan and follow it all the way to the finish line.

What do you think about to stay focused and race efficiently even when it feels like the wheels are about to come off? Surprisingly, you might want to think about your elbows. When everything hurts and your thighs or your calves are screaming for attention, divert your attention by focusing on a body part that doesn't hurt.

Another mental trick is to focus on the what got you to the starting line. Deena Kastor, American record holder in the marathon and half-marathon and Olympic bronze medalist, says that you can find confidence in your hard work. She reviews her training log before race day and finds conviction and credence in her earlier workouts.

To get through the marathon you need to call upon a higher power. For each of us, that means something different. Coach Andrew Kastor says that an event like the New York City Marathon offers inspiration everywhere you look.

Ryan Hall, American record holder in the half marathon, says that we should give thanks every time we run. Even bad workouts are a gift. The act of running alone is something to be cherished.

Andy Potts suggests finding inspiration and keeping it close when times are tough. He thinks of his children and strives to make them proud when self-doubt begins to creep in. His advice is simple and effective: "Smile through the sticky moments."

50 Race Day Tips for Your First Marathon

Congratulations on making it to the starting line after months of training. Here are some practical tips to help you run your very best on marathon race day. Good luck and Godspeed!

1. Plan your transportation to the starting area
2. Plan your transportation from the finish area
3. Pick a post-race meeting place for friends & family and write it the back of your bib
4. Run for a charity cause when possible
5. Drink coffee or tea, but no more than 2 cups before racing
6. Clip your toenails
7. Eat lots of carbs all week, switch to white pasta and breads 2 days before your race
8. No spicy food the day before
9. Make lunch your biggest meal the day before the race or eat dinner early
10. Pick out everything you'll wear, try it on, and set it out the night before
11. Pack a throwaway bag with snacks, fluids, and Vaseline to take to start
12. Don't wear new shoes

13. Wear the same type of gear you trained in. Be predictable.
14. Write your full name and emergency contact details on back of your bib
15. Pin your number to your shirt the night before
16. Go to bed early but read or watch TV if you can't sleep due to anxiety
17. Set more than one alarm clock and have a buddy call you just in case
18. Eat something like oatmeal and bananas in the morning, avoid fats
19. No massage the week before your race, no cross-training, be conservative
20. Sleep well the week before, night before isn't as crucial
21. Don't walk around sightseeing, save your legs for the marathon
22. Double knot your laces, but leave just a little room for your feet to swell
23. If it's cold bring gloves and hat from dollar store and throw away once you're warmed up
24. Bring toilet paper to the start
25. Bring a trash bag to the start to sit on
26. Bring a bottle of water or sports drink to sip, not guzzle, before the race starts

27. Use an extra pinch of salt on your food the week before
28. Wear warm clothes while waiting to start and leave them in charity bins
29. Being nervous is part of it, trust in your training and your taper
30. Visualize reaching your goal and crossing the finish with your arms raised in celebration
31. Drink a little bit at each water stop or at least rinse your mouth out
32. Only drink water with your energy gels
33. Avoid puddles, potholes, and curbs
34. Start at a slower pace than you hope to finish (negative splits)
35. Aim to run an even goal race pace if possible
36. Temperature, wind, and hills will make things harder and slower, adjust your expectations accordingly
37. Try to run the tangents when you go around corners, the distance adds up
38. Fatigue will visit you, be ready to kick it's ass when it does
39. During the last 6 miles, everybody hurts. This is what you signed up for.
40. Stand up straight, you'll breathe easier

41. Look where you're going and you'll get there faster, keep your head high
42. Listen to the crowd cheer and feed of their positive energy
43. Write your name on your shirt so people can cheer for YOU
44. Wear band-aids or something extra over your nipples to avoid chafing in wet conditions
45. Wear sunglasses to avoid squinting and stay relaxed
46. Put plenty of Vaseline on any hot spots before you start
47. Tape over existing blisters with band-aids and duct tape
48. Fuel the way you did during your long run training
49. Smile at the photographers, a picture is forever
50. High five the kids along the race course and enjoy the experience

Expert Tip: Use 5K split times for pacing, rather than mile splits. This will allow for variables such as elevation and congestion at the start.

6
Marathon Recovery

Congratulations! You did it. 99.5% of the American population will never know what that feels like. You are now, and forever, a member of the marathon tribe.

Your body is weak and your muscles are damaged. Pushing yourself too hard, too soon will result in injury. Recovering from your first marathon requires patience and attention.

1. Rest

You already showed the world what you can do. It's OK to dial things back and put your feet up for a little while. The first two days after the race you should not even think about putting your running shoes on. Maybe a little walk around the block or through the neighborhood to get the blood flowing, but nothing more. Try to get in bed early and let your body recover and rebuild.

2. Nutrition

You probably burned in excess of 3500 calories on race day and lost a few pounds between the start and the finish. Your body consumed all of your available fuel and then tapped into your reserves. Now is the time to restock the shelves with nutritious meals and plenty of water. You will feel better and have more energy if you keep the tank full with healthy snacks throughout the day. You may want to consider an immunity booster or extra vitamin C to keep your body protected during this time.

3. TLC

Icing sore muscles and joints, elevating your feet, and massaging your muscles will all help speed recovery and make you feel less like a stiff-legged zombie. Be careful not to do any kind of deep massage for at least several days after your marathon. Your muscles are still very tender and vulnerable. Even if you feel better, you are still a mess at the microscopic level.

4. Walking

Walking can be very therapeutic. It allows you to get outside and feel like your back in the routine again- albeit much slower. Cross-training activities like cycling and swimming are also a good forms of exercise to help keep your cardio levels high while reducing the stress on your overused muscles and joints. Whatever you choose, keep it easy and stay in the green zone for effort.

5. Backwards Taper

As you make your way back to regular training, think of it as a reverse taper. You are going to slowly build your mileage up in a way that will keep you healthy, reduce injury, and give you a solid foundation to build upon for the future.

Below is an example of a 3-week recovery plan following the marathon. Every runner will recover at their own rate, so your plan will need to be very flexible based on what your body is telling you. Don't push it, injuries will follow unless you're ready.

Day 1 – Rest and Recuperate, 2-3 15 minute walks

Day 2 – Rest and Recuperate, 2-3 15 minute walks

Day 3 – 2 Miles at a very easy pace

Day 4 – Rest and Recuperate, 2-3 15 minute walks

Day 5 – 3 Miles at a very easy pace

Day 6 – Rest and Recuperate, 2-3 15 minute walks

Day 7 – Rest and Recuperate, 2-3 15 minute walks

Day 8 – 3 Miles at a very easy pace

Day 9 – 3 Miles at a very easy pace

Day 10 – Rest and Recuperate, 2-3 15 minute walks

Day 11 – 5 Miles at a very easy pace

Day 12 – 5 Miles at a very easy pace

Day 13 – Rest

Day 14 – 6 Miles at a very easy pace

Day 15 – Rest

Day 16 – 6 Miles regular run

Day 17 – 3 Miles easy

Day 18 – 6 Miles regular run

Day 19 – 4 Miles easy

Day 20 – Rest

Day 21 – 10 Miles easy

During the recovery phase it's normal to feel a bit depressed. After 16 weeks of intense training and the thrill of your first marathon finish, your normal routine probably feels a little flat. This is a good time to count your blessings and recharge both mentally and physically before you start your next training phase.

Even the pros make it a habit to enjoy an extended period of total rest after the racing season is over. The wear and tear of training and racing effects both body and mind. Even the immune system and the hormonal system become compromised after months of hard training.

A healthy diet and plenty of sleep is crucial during this time. Your tired body is especially vulnerable to illness and respiratory infections after running a marathon. While you're sleeping, you can dream about running your next marathon.

Expert Tip: Your bed is your greatest recovery tool.

Thank You

I hope this guide has helped you train and prepare for your first marathon. All of the advice I've shared has been earned through experience. In your quest to become a better runner I hope that you visit SaltmarshRunning.com and subscribe to our mailing list for weekly tips and inspiring running stories.

Thank you for running. You never know who you might inspire when you're out there on your long training runs. Stay safe and enjoy the miles!

-Jason

Printed in Great Britain
by Amazon